MAD LIBS® after dark

MAD LIBS® after dark

Mad Libs
An Imprint of Penguin Random House

MAD LIBS
An Imprint of Penguin Random House LLC

Concept created by Roger Price & Leonard Stern

Mad Libs After Dark published in 2018 by Mad Libs,
an imprint of Penguin Random House LLC,
345 Hudson Street, New York, New York 10014.
Manufactured in China.

Mad Libs After Dark ISBN 9781524788681

3 5 7 9 10 8 6 4

INSTRUCTIONS

Adult MAD LIBS®
The world's greatest _dating_ game

MAD LIBS® is a game for people who don't like games!
It can be played by one, two, three, four, or forty.

• RIDICULOUSLY SIMPLE DIRECTIONS

In this book, you'll find stories containing blank spaces where words are left out. One player, the READER, selects one of the stories. The READER shouldn't tell anyone what the story is about. Instead, the READER should ask the other players, the WRITERS, to give words to fill in the blank spaces in the story.

• TO PLAY

The READER asks each WRITER in turn to call out words—adjectives or nouns or whatever the spaces call for—and uses them to fill in the blank spaces in the story. The result is your very own MAD LIBS! Then, when the READER reads the completed MAD LIBS to the other players, they will discover they have written a story that is fantastic, screamingly funny, shocking, silly, crazy, or just plain dumb— depending on the words each WRITER called out.

• EXAMPLE (*Before* and *After*)

"_____!" he said _____
            EXCLAMATION   ADVERB

as he jumped into his convertible _____ and
                                                            NOUN

drove off with his _____ wife.
                              ADJECTIVE

"_____*Ouch*_____!" he said _____*stupidly*_____
            EXCLAMATION   ADVERB

as he jumped into his convertible _____*cat*_____ and
                                                            NOUN

drove off with his _____*brave*_____ wife.
                              ADJECTIVE

Adult MAD LIBS®
The world's greatest _dating_ game

In case you have forgotten what adjectives, adverbs, nouns, and verbs are, here is a quick review:

An **ADJECTIVE** describes something or somebody. *Lumpy, soft, ugly, messy,* and *short* are adjectives.

An **ADVERB** tells how something is done. It modifies a verb and usually ends in "ly." *Modestly, stupidly, greedily,* and *carefully* are adverbs.

A **NOUN** is the name of a person, place, or thing. *Sidewalk, umbrella, bridle, bathtub,* and *nose* are nouns.

A **VERB** is an action word. *Run, pitch, jump,* and *swim* are verbs. Put the verbs in past tense if the directions say **PAST TENSE**. *Ran, pitched, jumped,* and *swam* are verbs in the past tense.

When we ask for **A PLACE**, we mean any sort of place: a country or city (*Spain, Cleveland*) or a room (*bathroom, kitchen*).

An **EXCLAMATION** or **SILLY WORD** is any sort of funny sound, gasp, grunt, or outcry, like *Wow!, Ouch!, Whomp!, Ick!,* and *Gadzooks!*

When we ask for specific words, like a **NUMBER**, a **COLOR**, an **ANIMAL**, or a **PART OF THE BODY**, we mean a word that is one of those things, like *seven, blue, horse,* or *head*.

When we ask for a **PLURAL**, it means more than one. For example, *cat* pluralized is *cats*.

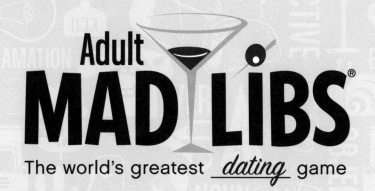

Adult MAD LIBS®

The world's greatest *dating* game

First Date Mad Libs

by Mickie Matheis

Mad Libs
An Imprint of Penguin Random House

MAD LIBS

WAYS TO MEET PEOPLE

The world's greatest _dating_ game

MAD LIBS® is fun to play with friends, but you can also play it by yourself! To begin with, DO NOT look at the story on the page below. Fill in the blanks on this page with the words called for. Then, using the words you have selected, fill in the blank spaces in the story. Now you've created your own hilarious MAD LIBS® game!

NOUN _____

A PLACE _____

ADJECTIVE _____

NOUN _____

NOUN _____

ANIMAL _____

VERB ENDING IN "ING" _____

PLURAL NOUN _____

PLURAL NOUN _____

ADJECTIVE _____

VERB _____

PLURAL NOUN _____

PLURAL NOUN _____

NOUN _____

VERB ENDING IN "ING" _____

NOUN _____

TYPE OF LIQUID _____

PLURAL NOUN _____

ARTICLE OF CLOTHING _____

ADJECTIVE _____

Where can you meet a nice, normal _____ to date? Sure, there
_____NOUN_____

are traditional avenues like the workplace or (the) _____, but
_____A PLACE____

here are some other creative, _____ ways:
_____ADJECTIVE_____

- Show off your sexy athletic skills by joining a/an _____-ball
_____NOUN_____

  team at a rec center.

- Walk your favorite four-legged _____ at the local _____ park.
_____NOUN_____ANIMAL___

- Attend a/an _____ class at a community college.
_____VERB ENDING IN "ING"___

- Look for antique _____ for your collection at a flea market.
_____PLURAL NOUN___

- Suggestively squeeze the largest, juiciest _____ while
_____PLURAL NOUN____

  exploring the _____ farmers' market.
_____ADJECTIVE___

- _____ with hundreds of other crazy _____ as part
__VERB_____PLURAL NOUN___

  of a flash mob.

- Volunteer to plant _____ at a neighborhood park.
_____PLURAL NOUN___

- Try daring, _____-defying new adventures like sky-_____.
_____NOUN_____VERB ENDING IN "ING"___

- Go to cultural events like _____ museums or _____ tastings.
_____NOUN_____TYPE OF LIQUID___

- Do cardio or lift _____ at the gym in your tightest
_____PLURAL NOUN___

  _____—you'll feel fit and look _____!
ARTICLE OF CLOTHING_____ADJECTIVE___

From ADULT MAD LIBS®: First Date Mad Libs • Copyright © 2013 by Penguin Random House LLC.

Adult MAD LIBS® SMACKDOWN

The world's greatest *dating* game

MAD LIBS® is fun to play with friends, but you can also play it by yourself! To begin with, DO NOT look at the story on the page below. Fill in the blanks on this page with the words called for. Then, using the words you have selected, fill in the blank spaces in the story. Now you've created your own hilarious MAD LIBS® game!

CELEBRITY _____

PERSON IN ROOM _____

NOUN _____

VERB ENDING IN "ING" _____

PART OF THE BODY (PLURAL) _____

NOUN _____

ADJECTIVE _____

PART OF THE BODY _____

ADJECTIVE _____

ADVERB _____

TYPE OF LIQUID _____

NOUN _____

ADVERB _____

ADJECTIVE _____

PLURAL NOUN _____

PART OF THE BODY (PLURAL) _____

NOUN _____

PLURAL NOUN _____

ADJECTIVE _____

NOUN _____

Adult MAD LIBS® SMACKDOWN

The world's greatest _dating_ game

He noticed her immediately. She had the beauty of _____

CELEBRITY

and the curves of _____. What was a gorgeous

PERSON IN ROOM

_____ like her doing _____ all alone at this party,

NOUN VERB ENDING IN "ING"

anyway? When their _____ locked across the crowded

PART OF THE BODY (PLURAL)

_____, a/an _____ smile slowly crept across her

NOUN ADJECTIVE

_____. The _____ chemistry seemed undeniable.

PART OF THE BODY ADJECTIVE

It was _____ obvious that she wanted him. He grabbed

ADVERB

two glasses of bubbly _____ from the tray of a passing

TYPE OF LIQUID

_____ and strode _____ across the room. Her smile

NOUN ADVERB

grew bigger the closer he got. He felt confident and _____.

ADJECTIVE

He imagined their first date—a candlelit dinner at La Maison de

_____, all _____ turning when he walked in with

PLURAL NOUN PART OF THE BODY (PLURAL)

this stunning _____ on his arm. He would dazzle her with

NOUN

witty _____ and _____ charm. "So what was the first

PLURAL NOUN ADJECTIVE

thing you noticed about me?" he said upon reaching her. She batted

her eyelashes and replied: "Your _____ is unzipped."

NOUN

Adult MAD LIBS

GLAMMING IT UP

The world's greatest *dating* game

MAD LIBS® is fun to play with friends, but you can also play it by yourself! To begin with, DO NOT look at the story on the page below. Fill in the blanks on this page with the words called for. Then, using the words you have selected, fill in the blank spaces in the story. Now you've created your own hilarious MAD LIBS® game!

PERSON IN ROOM _____

PERSON IN ROOM _____

ADJECTIVE _____

PLURAL NOUN _____

A PLACE _____

ADVERB _____

ADJECTIVE _____

NOUN _____

ADJECTIVE _____

PART OF THE BODY (PLURAL) _____

CELEBRITY _____

NOUN _____

COLOR _____

PART OF THE BODY (PLURAL) _____

PART OF THE BODY _____

NUMBER _____

ADJECTIVE _____

NOUN _____

TYPE OF FOOD _____

TYPE OF FOOD _____

ADJECTIVE _____

ADJECTIVE _____

Adult
MAD LIBS®
The world's greatest _dating_ game **GLAMMING IT UP**

_____ had been looking forward to her first date with
_{PERSON IN ROOM}

_____ all week. He was a/an _____ catch! He
_{PERSON IN ROOM}   _{ADJECTIVE}

had his own business importing rare fossilized _____ from
_{PLURAL NOUN}

remote locations in (the) _____. He had to be _____
_{A PLACE}   _{ADVERB}

successful, because he drove a/an _____ sports car and
_{ADJECTIVE}

lived in a huge brick _____ in an upscale, _____
_{NOUN}   _{ADJECTIVE}

neighborhood. To top it off, his _____ were as finely
_{PART OF THE BODY (PLURAL)}

chiseled as _____'s. She grabbed her favorite low-cut
_{CELEBRITY}

_____ from the closet—it really brought out the _____
_{NOUN}   _{COLOR}

in her _____! Even better, it accented her ample
_{PART OF THE BODY (PLURAL)}

_____. She grabbed a pair of _____-inch stiletto
_{PART OF THE BODY}   _{NUMBER}

pumps and accessorized the outfit with a simple _____
_{ADJECTIVE}

pendant and an oversize pair of _____-shaped earrings.
_{NOUN}

To make sure she got all his senses tingling, she sprayed on her best

_____-scented perfume and used some _____-flavored
_{TYPE OF FOOD}   _{TYPE OF FOOD}

breath freshener. _You're as_ _____ _as you'll ever be,_ she thought.
_{ADJECTIVE}

Now get out there and knock him _____!
_{ADJECTIVE}

Adult MAD LIBS

STRIKE THOSE QUESTIONS

The world's greatest *dating* game

MAD LIBS® is fun to play with friends, but you can also play it by yourself! To begin with, DO NOT look at the story on the page below. Fill in the blanks on this page with the words called for. Then, using the words you have selected, fill in the blank spaces in the story. Now you've created your own hilarious MAD LIBS® game!

ADVERB _____

NOUN _____

ADJECTIVE _____

ADJECTIVE _____

A PLACE _____

ADJECTIVE _____

PLURAL NOUN _____

PART OF THE BODY (PLURAL) _____

PLURAL NOUN _____

VERB (PAST TENSE) _____

ADJECTIVE _____

NOUN _____

ADJECTIVE _____

NOUN _____

VERB _____

NOUN _____

Adult

MAD LIBS®

STRIKE THOSE QUESTIONS

The world's greatest _dating_ game

First dates are _____ awkward! You want to ask the good-
ADVERB

looking _____ sitting across from you a thousand things—
NOUN

but avoid asking questions that are far too _____, such as:
ADJECTIVE

- How much do you make at your _____ job?
ADJECTIVE

- What do you think about going to (the) _____ for
A PLACE

  our honeymoon?

- I want a big, _____ family. How many _____
ADJECTIVE   PLURAL NOUN

  do you want?

- Do you floss your _____ regularly?
PART OF THE BODY (PLURAL)

- So how many _____ have you _____ with?
PLURAL NOUN   VERB (PAST TENSE)

- Do you have any _____ tattoos on your _____?
ADJECTIVE   NOUN

- Where have you been all my _____ life? You're the
ADJECTIVE

  _____ I've been waiting for!
NOUN

- Do you _____ on the first date?
VERB

- (Depending on the answer to the question above) . . .

  Your _____ or mine?
NOUN

MAD LIBS® is fun to play with friends, but you can also play it by yourself! To begin with, DO NOT look at the story on the page below. Fill in the blanks on this page with the words called for. Then, using the words you have selected, fill in the blank spaces in the story. Now you've created your own hilarious MAD LIBS® game!

NOUN _____

ADJECTIVE _____

PLURAL NOUN _____

PART OF THE BODY_____

PLURAL NOUN _____

ADJECTIVE _____

ADJECTIVE _____

NOUN _____

ADVERB _____

A PLACE _____

ADJECTIVE _____

NOUN _____

ARTICLE OF CLOTHING (PLURAL) _____

PART OF THE BODY (PLURAL) _____

VERB ENDING IN "ING"_____

ADJECTIVE _____

PLURAL NOUN _____

NOUN _____

ADJECTIVE _____

PART OF THE BODY_____

ADJECTIVE _____

PLURAL NOUN _____

Adult MAD LIBS®

ROMANTIC MEN

The world's greatest _dating_ game

What type of leading _____ gets you all hot and _____?
                        NOUN   ADJECTIVE

Do you prefer brains over _____? Do you like a scruffy
                            PLURAL NOUN

_____ versus a clean-shaven look? Ahh—so many _____,
PART OF THE BODY   PLURAL NOUN

so little time! Let's look at what's on the _____ menu:
                                             ADJECTIVE

- The _____ professional who wears a three-piece
        ADJECTIVE

  _____ and strides _____ through the streets
   NOUN   ADVERB

  of (the) _____, ready to close the next _____ deal
            A PLACE   ADJECTIVE

- The blue-collar _____ who knocks around in jeans,
                    NOUN

  boots, and flannel _____, and can fix or build
                      ARTICLE OF CLOTHING (PLURAL)

  anything with his own two _____
                             PART OF THE BODY (PLURAL)

- The intellectual, _____ man who contemplates
                      VERB ENDING IN "ING"

  _____ questions like "Why are we here?" and "What
   ADJECTIVE

  is the meaning of _____?"
                      PLURAL NOUN

- The artistic _____ who is quiet, sensitive, and
                NOUN

  _____. He has a creative _____ and can see the
   ADJECTIVE   PART OF THE BODY

  beauty in everything from a/an _____ flower garden to
                                  ADJECTIVE

  a pile of rotting _____.
                     PLURAL NOUN

Adult MAD LIBS®

FANTASY FIRST DATES: PART 1

The world's greatest *dating* game

MAD LIBS® is fun to play with friends, but you can also play it by yourself! To begin with, DO NOT look at the story on the page below. Fill in the blanks on this page with the words called for. Then, using the words you have selected, fill in the blank spaces in the story. Now you've created your own hilarious MAD LIBS® game!

PLURAL NOUN _____

NOUN _____

A PLACE _____

NOUN _____

NUMBER _____

NOUN _____

ADJECTIVE _____

NUMBER _____

TYPE OF LIQUID _____

ADJECTIVE _____

NOUN _____

NOUN _____

ADJECTIVE _____

VERB ENDING IN "ING" _____

PLURAL NOUN _____

ADJECTIVE _____

VERB ENDING IN "ING" _____

NOUN _____

The best first dates involve grand romantic _____ like these:

PLURAL NOUN

- Charter a private _____ and fly to (the) _____—also

NOUN   A PLACE

  known as the _____ of Love—for a/an _____-course dinner

NOUN   NUMBER

  followed by a moonlit ride in a/an _____ along the canals.

NOUN

- Prepare a/an _____ gourmet picnic complete with

ADJECTIVE

  a/an _____-dollar bottle of _____ and a quartet

NUMBER   TYPE OF LIQUID

  serenading you with _____ songs.

ADJECTIVE

- Rent a space on the Jumbo-_____ during a/an

NOUN

  _____-ball game and post a super-_____ message

NOUN   ADJECTIVE

  like _Glad we're_ _____ _together here today!_

VERB ENDING IN "ING"

- Send a bouquet of long-stemmed red _____ before

PLURAL NOUN

  and after the date—and for good measure, send one to the

  _____ restaurant where you're wining and _____

ADJECTIVE   VERB ENDING IN "ING"

  your date.

- Take a nighttime hot-air _____ ride to check out the stars.

NOUN

Adult MAD LIBS®

DATING DISASTERS

The world's greatest _dating_ game

MAD LIBS® is fun to play with friends, but you can also play it by yourself! To begin with, DO NOT look at the story on the page below. Fill in the blanks on this page with the words called for. Then, using the words you have selected, fill in the blank spaces in the story. Now you've created your own hilarious MAD LIBS® game!

ADJECTIVE _____

ADJECTIVE _____

PLURAL NOUN _____

PLURAL NOUN _____

ADJECTIVE _____

PERSON IN ROOM _____

PART OF THE BODY (PLURAL) _____

VERB _____

PART OF THE BODY _____

ADJECTIVE _____

ADJECTIVE _____

SILLY WORD _____

ADJECTIVE _____

PART OF THE BODY (PLURAL) _____

CELEBRITY _____

PERSON IN ROOM _____

Adult MAD LIBS® — DATING DISASTERS

The world's greatest _dating_ game

Ever have a/an _____ first date where you can't believe
ADJECTIVE

you wasted more than five minutes with such an unbelievably

_____ person? Listen to these _____ recount their
ADJECTIVE   PLURAL NOUN

most memorable first-date disasters:

Taylor: A guy once cooked pasta with _____ for me,
PLURAL NOUN

but when he was serving it, he "accidentally" spilled it all over my

_____ shirt—then suggested he eat it off me.
ADJECTIVE

Emma: I went out with this beast named _____
PERSON IN ROOM

who showed up in an "I like big _____ and I cannot
PART OF THE BODY (PLURAL)

_____" T-shirt. She said that was why she was attracted to
VERB

me—because my _____ was so big and _____!
PART OF THE BODY   ADJECTIVE

Priya: I will never forget this _____ guy named
ADJECTIVE

_____. He looked like a male model—with long,
SILLY WORD

_____ hair and a pair of rock-hard _____ that
ADJECTIVE   PART OF THE BODY (PLURAL)

he nicknamed _____ and _____.
CELEBRITY   PERSON IN ROOM

Adult MAD LIBS®

The world's greatest _dating_ game

FIRST-DATE DEAL BREAKERS: FOR MEN

MAD LIBS® is fun to play with friends, but you can also play it by yourself! To begin with, DO NOT look at the story on the page below. Fill in the blanks on this page with the words called for. Then, using the words you have selected, fill in the blank spaces in the story. Now you've created your own hilarious MAD LIBS® game!

NOUN _____

NOUN _____

NOUN _____

ADJECTIVE _____

NOUN _____

PLURAL NOUN _____

VERB ENDING IN "ING" _____

COLOR _____

NOUN _____

ADJECTIVE _____

A PLACE _____

A PLACE _____

CELEBRITY _____

NOUN _____

Adult
MAD LIBS®

FIRST-DATE DEAL BREAKERS: FOR MEN

The world's greatest _dating_ game

Even if she's the prettiest, coolest _____ you've ever been
                                           NOUN

out with, there will be no second date if she does any of these

off-the-_____ things:
          NOUN

- Shows up in a/an _____-encrusted tiara, calls you
                          NOUN

  her _____ servant, and says she deserves to be treated like
         ADJECTIVE

  a royal _____
            NOUN

- Says she likes it when good-looking _____ chase after her,
                                            PLURAL NOUN

  then proceeds to take off _____ and yells for you to catch her.
                                VERB ENDING IN "ING"

- Starts talking about whether her wedding dress should be white

  or off-_____ and assures you that she likes _____
           COLOR   NOUN

  rings just as much as diamond ones

- Admits that although she would prefer a/an _____
                                                   ADJECTIVE

  vacation home in (the) _____, she could live with one
                             A PLACE

  in (the) _____
              A PLACE

- Confesses that she thought you looked like _____,
                                                    CELEBRITY

  but that up close, you actually resemble a pug-faced _____
                                                              NOUN

Adult MAD LIBS

The world's greatest _dating_ game

MAD LIBS® is fun to play with friends, but you can also play it by yourself! To begin with, DO NOT look at the story on the page below. Fill in the blanks on this page with the words called for. Then, using the words you have selected, fill in the blank spaces in the story. Now you've created your own hilarious MAD LIBS® game!

NOUN _____

ADJECTIVE _____

VERB ENDING IN "ING" _____

PART OF THE BODY _____

ADJECTIVE _____

PART OF THE BODY (PLURAL) _____

TYPE OF FOOD _____

NOUN _____

NOUN _____

NOUN _____

ARTICLE OF CLOTHING _____

NOUN _____

ADJECTIVE _____

PART OF THE BODY _____

Adult MAD LIBS®

The world's greatest *dating* game

FIRST-DATE DEAL BREAKERS: FOR WOMEN

Could he be the _____ of your dreams? The _____
                        NOUN   ADJECTIVE

man you were meant to be with forever? Maybe—but he's not worth

a second date if he:

- Shows up at your door looking, smelling, and _____
                                                   VERB ENDING IN "ING"

  better than you.

- Checks out his _____ while walking by storefront windows
                    PART OF THE BODY

- Promises you an evening that will be a "blast"—and takes you

  back to his _____ place to play a video game where you
               ADJECTIVE

  blow off your opponents' _____
                            PART OF THE BODY (PLURAL)

- Exudes an inexplicable odor of day-old _____
                                           TYPE OF FOOD

- Pulls up to your place on a two-wheeled _____ and
                                            NOUN

  honks his _____ to announce his arrival
             NOUN

- Asks you to pay the bill because he left his _____ in his
                                                 NOUN

  other _____
         ARTICLE OF CLOTHING

- Gives you a lovely gold _____—and says how everyone
                           NOUN

  he dates seem to like it

- Invites you to feel how _____ and muscular his _____ is
                          ADJECTIVE   PART OF THE BODY

Adult MAD LIBS® FLIRTING 101

The world's greatest _dating_ game

MAD LIBS® is fun to play with friends, but you can also play it by yourself! To begin with, DO NOT look at the story on the page below. Fill in the blanks on this page with the words called for. Then, using the words you have selected, fill in the blank spaces in the story. Now you've created your own hilarious MAD LIBS® game!

PART OF THE BODY (PLURAL) _____

ADJECTIVE _____

NOUN _____

NOUN _____

ADJECTIVE _____

NOUN _____

VERB _____

VERB ENDING IN "ING" _____

ADJECTIVE _____

ADJECTIVE _____

PART OF THE BODY _____

NOUN _____

ADJECTIVE _____

ADVERB _____

PART OF THE BODY _____

NOUN _____

PART OF THE BODY _____

Adult MAD LIBS® FLIRTING 101

The world's greatest _dating_ game

If you're determined to land that first date, you must occasionally

take matters into your own _____ . Sometimes a little
_{PART OF THE BODY (PLURAL)}

_____ flirting is all you need to get that hot _____
ADJECTIVE   NOUN

following you around like a lovesick _____! Once
NOUN

you've identified your _____ target, cast a come-hither
ADJECTIVE

_____ that says, "I would like to _____ you—
NOUN   VERB

right here and now." Close the distance between the two of you

by _____ in your most seductive, _____ manner
VERB ENDING IN "ING"   ADJECTIVE

across the floor. Engage your beloved in some _____
ADJECTIVE

conversation. Appear totally into them by nodding your _____
PART OF THE BODY

at whatever they say, as if you are hanging on their every _____.
NOUN

If they say something _____, laugh _____ and
ADJECTIVE   ADVERB

lightly touch their _____. If you make your crush feel like
PART OF THE BODY

the only _____ in the room, they'll be eating out of your
NOUN

_____ in no time.
PART OF THE BODY

Adult MAD LIBS®

The world's greatest _dating_ game

THANKS, BUT NO THANKS

MAD LIBS® is fun to play with friends, but you can also play it by yourself! To begin with, DO NOT look at the story on the page below. Fill in the blanks on this page with the words called for. Then, using the words you have selected, fill in the blank spaces in the story. Now you've created your own hilarious MAD LIBS® game!

NOUN _____

PLURAL NOUN _____

A PLACE _____

PLURAL NOUN _____

EXCLAMATION _____

NOUN _____

NOUN _____

VERB _____

SAME VERB _____

ADJECTIVE _____

PERSON IN ROOM _____

NOUN _____

ADJECTIVE _____

PART OF THE BODY _____

ADJECTIVE _____

PLURAL NOUN _____

Adult MAD LIBS®

The world's greatest _dating_ game

THANKS, BUT NO THANKS

You're flattered when a nice _____ asks you out, but
                              NOUN

when it comes to _____ who think they are king of (the)
                  PLURAL NOUN

_____, there's nothing more satisfying than sending them off
A PLACE

with their _____ tucked between their legs with responses like:
            PLURAL NOUN

- Not only no—but _____ no!
                   EXCLAMATION

- I would rather go out with an inflatable _____.
                                           NOUN

- I wouldn't date you if you were the last _____ on earth.
                                           NOUN

- This is a do-or-_____ situation—and frankly, I'd prefer
                  VERB

  to _____.
     SAME VERB

- Sorry, I have pretty _____ standards, but you don't even
                       ADJECTIVE

  meet those.

- Well, you do remind me of my cousin _____. The only
                                      PERSON IN ROOM

  trouble is, I can't stand that _____.
                                 NOUN

- You have a nice face, but I'm really turned off by your

  _____ _____.
  ADJECTIVE   PART OF THE BODY

- Yes, I would love to go out with you—when you're good-looking,

  _____, and have a net worth of one million _____.
  ADJECTIVE   PLURAL NOUN

Adult MAD LIBS

ONLINE PERSONALITY PROFILE

The world's greatest *dating* game

MAD LIBS® is fun to play with friends, but you can also play it by yourself! To begin with, DO NOT look at the story on the page below. Fill in the blanks on this page with the words called for. Then, using the words you have selected, fill in the blank spaces in the story. Now you've created your own hilarious MAD LIBS® game!

PERSON IN ROOM _____

ADJECTIVE _____

VERB _____

NOUN _____

ADJECTIVE _____

VERB _____

VERB _____

NOUN _____

CELEBRITY _____

PART OF THE BODY (PLURAL) _____

COLOR _____

COLOR _____

ADJECTIVE _____

PART OF THE BODY _____

NUMBER _____

VERB ENDING IN "ING" _____

ADJECTIVE _____

TYPE OF FOOD (PLURAL) _____

ANIMAL _____

A PLACE _____

NOUN _____

VERB _____

Adult MAD LIBS

ONLINE PERSONALITY PROFILE

The world's greatest *dating* game

Well hello, potential suitors! My name is _____,
PERSON IN ROOM

and I'm on the lookout for a fun, _____, and handsome
ADJECTIVE

companion to _____ with morning, noon, and night!
VERB

Want to know more about me? I'm a bubbly kind of _____.
NOUN

I'm adventurous, daring, and _____-go-lucky. I hop,
ADJECTIVE

skip, and _____ for joy *just because I can*! I'm independent
VERB

and _____ to the beat of my own drum. No one tells
VERB

this _____ what to do! What do I look like, you ask?
NOUN

Are you familiar with the awesome _____? Well,
CELEBRITY

people will say our _____ look totally alike, but that's
PART OF THE BODY (PLURAL)

where the similarities end! My hair is _____, my eyes
COLOR

are light _____, and I have a/an _____-licious
COLOR   ADJECTIVE

_____. On a scale of one to ten, I would rate myself
PART OF THE BODY

a/an _____ and a half. I enjoy _____ for exercise;
NUMBER   VERB ENDING IN "ING"

following my favorite band, _____ _____;
ADJECTIVE   TYPE OF FOOD (PLURAL)

and _____-watching in the forests of (the) _____.
ANIMAL   A PLACE

If I sound like the _____ for you, _____ today!
NOUN   VERB

Adult MAD LIBS®

The world's greatest *dating* game

LET'S GET COOKIN'

MAD LIBS® is fun to play with friends, but you can also play it by yourself! To begin with, DO NOT look at the story on the page below. Fill in the blanks on this page with the words called for. Then, using the words you have selected, fill in the blank spaces in the story. Now you've created your own hilarious MAD LIBS® game!

ADJECTIVE _____

NOUN _____

PERSON IN ROOM _____

NOUN _____

PLURAL NOUN _____

ADJECTIVE _____

PLURAL NOUN _____

ADJECTIVE _____

TYPE OF LIQUID _____

TYPE OF LIQUID _____

PLURAL NOUN _____

NOUN _____

COLOR _____

COLOR _____

PLURAL NOUN _____

ADJECTIVE _____

CELEBRITY _____

ADVERB _____

PLURAL NOUN _____

PLURAL NOUN _____

ADJECTIVE _____

NOUN _____

Adult
MAD LIBS® LET'S GET COOKIN'

The world's greatest _dating_ game

One of the most tried-and-_____ ways to impress a first
                              ADJECTIVE

date is to plan and cook a romantic _____, so that's
                                            NOUN

what _____ decided to do. He began to prepare a seared
        PERSON IN ROOM

_____ seasoned with ground _____ and dried
      NOUN   PLURAL NOUN

_____ herbs. He whipped up some mashed _____
   ADJECTIVE   PLURAL NOUN

and made a bowl of mixed _____ greens tossed with a
                              ADJECTIVE

light dressing of olive oil and _____. He poured some
                                  TYPE OF LIQUID

fine red _____ into a pair of crystal _____, lit
           TYPE OF LIQUID   PLURAL NOUN

a few _____-scented candles, and arranged some
          NOUN

lovely _____ and _____ _____
          COLOR   COLOR   PLURAL NOUN

in a vase in the center of the table. _What's missing?_ he wondered.

Right—some _____ _mood music!_ He pulled out his favorite
                ADJECTIVE

_____ CD and turned it on _____ in the
   CELEBRITY   ADVERB

background. Then he fluffed the _____ on the couch and set
                                    PLURAL NOUN

out a bowl of after-dinner _____. Would his date notice all
                              PLURAL NOUN

his _____ efforts? Only time—and a passionate good-night
      ADJECTIVE

_____—would tell!
      NOUN

Adult MAD LIBS® ALL THE RIGHT MOVES

The world's greatest _dating_ game

MAD LIBS® is fun to play with friends, but you can also play it by yourself! To begin with, DO NOT look at the story on the page below. Fill in the blanks on this page with the words called for. Then, using the words you have selected, fill in the blank spaces in the story. Now you've created your own hilarious MAD LIBS® game!

EXCLAMATION _____

PERSON IN ROOM _____

ADJECTIVE _____

PLURAL NOUN _____

TYPE OF LIQUID _____

NOUN _____

NOUN _____

NOUN _____

ADJECTIVE _____

A PLACE _____

VERB (PAST TENSE) _____

ADJECTIVE _____

NOUN _____

NOUN _____

ADJECTIVE _____

SILLY WORD _____

ARTICLE OF CLOTHING (PLURAL) _____

TYPE OF LIQUID _____

VERB (PAST TENSE) _____

COLOR _____

NOUN _____

ADJECTIVE _____

Adult MAD LIBS® ALL THE RIGHT MOVES

The world's greatest _dating_ game

"_____!" was all _____ could say. Her date
    EXCLAMATION   PERSON IN ROOM

that night was nothing short of _____. He had brought
                        ADJECTIVE

her a bouquet of fragrant _____. Once she put them in
                   PLURAL NOUN

some _____, he helped her put on her _____.
    TYPE OF LIQUID   NOUN

They walked out to his pickup _____, where he held the
                        NOUN

_____ open for her. He had made reservations at a/an
   NOUN

_____ restaurant in a fancy part of (the) _____.
ADJECTIVE   A PLACE

They _____ all throughout dinner—they had so many
    VERB (PAST TENSE)

_____ things in common! Like a true gentle-_____,
ADJECTIVE   NOUN

he picked up the entire bill, and she noticed he left a very generous

_____ for the waiter. He asked if she'd like to go for a walk
   NOUN

along the beach since it was a/an _____, moonlit night, and
                     ADJECTIVE

she said, "_____!" They kicked off their _____,
       SILLY WORD   ARTICLE OF CLOTHING (PLURAL)

dipped their bare toes in the cool blue _____, and
                     TYPE OF LIQUID

_____ for the first time. Finally she whispered the words any
VERB (PAST TENSE)

_____-blooded man loves to hear: "Is that a/an _____
  COLOR   NOUN

in your pocket, or are you just _____ to see me?"
                    ADJECTIVE

Adult MAD LIBS®

The world's greatest *dating* game

FIRST-DATE ADVICE

MAD LIBS® is fun to play with friends, but you can also play it by yourself! To begin with, DO NOT look at the story on the page below. Fill in the blanks on this page with the words called for. Then, using the words you have selected, fill in the blank spaces in the story. Now you've created your own hilarious MAD LIBS® game!

ADJECTIVE _____

VERB ENDING IN "ING" _____

ADJECTIVE _____

PLURAL NOUN _____

NOUN _____

NOUN _____

ADVERB _____

ADJECTIVE _____

PERSON IN ROOM _____

CELEBRITY _____

NOUN _____

PLURAL NOUN _____

VERB _____

NOUN _____

Adult MAD LIBS®

The world's greatest *dating* game

FIRST-DATE ADVICE

A first date will either have you seeing _____ fireworks or
ADJECTIVE

_____ for your life! Either way, you need to be prepared.
VERB ENDING IN "ING"

Here are some _____ tips:
ADJECTIVE

- Have some extra _____ in case you have to catch
  PLURAL NOUN

  a/an _____ ride home.
  NOUN

- Make sure you have your cell _____ with you and it's
  NOUN

  _____ charged—but don't keep checking it for
  ADVERB

  _____ messages.
  ADJECTIVE

- If it's a blind date, don't hold it against them if they look more

  like _____ than, say, _____ .
  PERSON IN ROOM   CELEBRITY

- Dress appropriately—for example, if you're going _____
  NOUN

  climbing, don't wear tight pants and dress _____ .
  PLURAL NOUN

- Don't let them think you'll _____ on the first date—
  VERB

  because a proper _____ doesn't do that.
  NOUN

Adult MAD LIBS®

MADE FOR EACH OTHER?

The world's greatest _dating_ game

MAD LIBS® is fun to play with friends, but you can also play it by yourself! To begin with, DO NOT look at the story on the page below. Fill in the blanks on this page with the words called for. Then, using the words you have selected, fill in the blank spaces in the story. Now you've created your own hilarious MAD LIBS® game!

ADJECTIVE _____

VERB ENDING IN "ING" _____

VERB ENDING IN "ING" _____

NOUN _____

NOUN _____

NOUN _____

ADJECTIVE _____

VERB _____

NOUN _____

NUMBER _____

PLURAL NOUN _____

ADJECTIVE _____

VERB _____

PLURAL NOUN _____

ADJECTIVE _____

NOUN _____

VERB _____

Adult MAD LIBS® — MADE FOR EACH OTHER?

The world's greatest *dating* game

Can you know after just one _____ date if a person is the one

ADJECTIVE

you've been _____ for your whole life? If you agree on most

VERB ENDING IN "ING"

of these things, then you may eventually find yourself _____

VERB ENDING IN "ING"

down the aisle together:

- It doesn't matter who makes more money at their _____—

NOUN

  as long as you can both afford _____ .

NOUN

- Either spouse can be a stay-at-home _____.

NOUN

- A/An _____ partner should know how to cook, clean,

ADJECTIVE

  and _____ .

VERB

- Only buy as big of a/an _____ as you can afford.

NOUN

- Always have at least _____ _____ in the bank for

NUMBER PLURAL NOUN

  a/an _____ day.

ADJECTIVE

- Friends come and _____ , but family _____

VERB PLURAL NOUN

  are forever.

- Never go to bed _____.

ADJECTIVE

- "For richer, for poorer, in sickness and in health, until

  _____ do us part" are words to _____ by.

NOUN VERB

MAD LIBS® is fun to play with friends, but you can also play it by yourself! To begin with, DO NOT look at the story on the page below. Fill in the blanks on this page with the words called for. Then, using the words you have selected, fill in the blank spaces in the story. Now you've created your own hilarious MAD LIBS® game!

NOUN _____

ADJECTIVE _____

ADJECTIVE _____

VERB ENDING IN "ING" _____

NOUN _____

TYPE OF LIQUID _____

ADJECTIVE _____

PLURAL NOUN _____

ADJECTIVE _____

NOUN _____

NOUN _____

PART OF THE BODY (PLURAL) _____

PLURAL NOUN _____

VERB _____

PLURAL NOUN _____

VERB ENDING IN "ING" _____

ADJECTIVE _____

PART OF THE BODY _____

Adult MAD LIBS®

FUN AND FLIRTY FIRST DATES

The world's greatest _dating_ game

Most people still go the dinner-and-a/an-_____ route

NOUN

on the first date. Why not try something different? Here are some

_____ ideas that provide an equal blend of _____

ADJECTIVE   _ADJECTIVE_

conversation and casual _____:

VERB ENDING IN "ING"

- A bowling _____ is a fun place to enjoy a pitcher

  NOUN

  of _____, some _____ competition, and a stylish

  TYPE OF LIQUID   _ADJECTIVE_

  pair of _____ for your feet.

  PLURAL NOUN

- A hike in the _____ outdoors is a breath of fresh

  ADJECTIVE

  _____—literally! Just make sure your date is not

  NOUN

  a high-maintenance _____ with perfectly manicured

  NOUN

  _____.

  PART OF THE BODY (PLURAL)

- A show at the theater lets you get dressed up in your best

  _____ and _____ at intermission, and is perfect

  PLURAL NOUN   _VERB_

  for those who enjoy books and artistic _____.

  PLURAL NOUN

- An afternoon at the _____ range lets you get up close

  VERB ENDING IN "ING"

  and _____—especially if you have to wrap your arms

  ADJECTIVE

  around your date's _____ to help with their golf swing.

  PART OF THE BODY

Adult
MAD LIBS
PICKUP LINES
The world's greatest *dating* game

MAD LIBS® is fun to play with friends, but you can also play it by yourself! To begin with, DO NOT look at the story on the page below. Fill in the blanks on this page with the words called for. Then, using the words you have selected, fill in the blank spaces in the story. Now you've created your own hilarious MAD LIBS® game!

ADVERB _____

ADJECTIVE _____

PART OF THE BODY _____

PLURAL NOUN _____

ADJECTIVE _____

PART OF THE BODY _____

ADJECTIVE _____

ADJECTIVE _____

NOUN _____

VERB _____

PART OF THE BODY _____

VERB ENDING IN "ING" _____

ADJECTIVE _____

NOUN _____

NOUN _____

ADJECTIVE _____

If you're _____ into someone and would like a/an _____
_{ADVERB} ADJECTIVE

date, wear your _____ on your sleeve when you ask them
PART OF THE BODY

out—and avoid cheesy pickup _____ like:
PLURAL NOUN

- Got a/an _____ bandage? I scraped my _____
  ADJECTIVE PART OF THE BODY

  falling for you.

- If being _____ were a crime, you'd be _____
  ADJECTIVE ADJECTIVE

  as charged!

- Do you believe in _____ at first sight—or should I
  NOUN

  _____ by you again?
  VERB

- Is your father a mechanic? How did you get such a finely tuned

  _____?
  PART OF THE BODY

- You must be tired after _____ through my mind all day.
  VERB ENDING IN "ING"

- I was so enchanted by your _____ beauty that I ran into
  ADJECTIVE

  that _____ over there. So I'll need your name and
  NOUN

  number for insurance purposes.

- If you were a laser _____, you'd be set on "stunning."
  NOUN

- Is it _____ in here—or is it just you?
  ADJECTIVE

Adult MAD LIBS®

The world's greatest _dating_ game

DATING DOS AND DON'TS

MAD LIBS® is fun to play with friends, but you can also play it by yourself! To begin with, DO NOT look at the story on the page below. Fill in the blanks on this page with the words called for. Then, using the words you have selected, fill in the blank spaces in the story. Now you've created your own hilarious MAD LIBS® game!

ADJECTIVE _____

ADJECTIVE _____

PLURAL NOUN _____

VERB _____

PLURAL NOUN _____

ADJECTIVE _____

PART OF THE BODY (PLURAL) _____

ADVERB _____

VERB ENDING IN "ING" _____

PART OF THE BODY _____

SILLY WORD _____

PART OF THE BODY _____

NOUN _____

TYPE OF LIQUID _____

PLURAL NOUN _____

ADJECTIVE _____

PART OF THE BODY _____

Adult MAD LIBS®
The world's greatest *dating* game

DATING DOS AND DON'TS

How do you make sure that first _____ date becomes a

ADJECTIVE

second _____ date? By following these helpful _____

ADJECTIVE — PLURAL NOUN

for what to do and what not to _____:

VERB

- **Don't** talk about your ex-_____.

PLURAL NOUN

- **Do** be confident and _____!

ADJECTIVE

- **Don't** cross your _____—it makes you seem

PART OF THE BODY (PLURAL)

  _____ uninterested in what your date is _____.

ADVERB — VERB ENDING IN "ING"

- **Do** be a good listener—lean in, nod your _____,

PART OF THE BODY

  and occasionally say, "_____."

SILLY WORD

- **Don't** end the date with anything other than a/an

  _____-shake.

PART OF THE BODY

- **Do** greet your date with a warm, sincere _____.

NOUN

- **Don't** drink too much _____ or you will start to slur

TYPE OF LIQUID

  your _____.

PLURAL NOUN

- **Do** be engaging, attentive, and _____.

ADJECTIVE

- **Don't** ogle the person's _____—even if it's the best

PART OF THE BODY

  you've ever seen!

MAD LIBS® is fun to play with friends, but you can also play it by yourself! To begin with, DO NOT look at the story on the page below. Fill in the blanks on this page with the words called for. Then, using the words you have selected, fill in the blank spaces in the story. Now you've created your own hilarious MAD LIBS® game!

PART OF THE BODY _____

ADJECTIVE _____

NOUN _____

ADJECTIVE _____

VERB ENDING IN "ING" _____

ADJECTIVE _____

VERB ENDING IN "ING" _____

ANIMAL (PLURAL) _____

NOUN _____

PLURAL NOUN _____

NOUN _____

A PLACE _____

NOUN _____

NOUN _____

PERSON IN ROOM _____

VERB _____

ADJECTIVE _____

TYPE OF LIQUID _____

PLURAL NOUN _____

Want to sweep your date off their _____? Here are a few
PART OF THE BODY

fantasy date ideas:

- Send your date a/an _____ satin _____ and
  ADJECTIVE   NOUN

  rent out a/an _____ ballroom for private _____ lessons.
  ADJECTIVE   VERB ENDING IN "ING"

- Cash in your retirement account to fund a/an _____
  ADJECTIVE

  private concert with your date's favorite band, _____
  VERB ENDING IN "ING"

  _____.
  ANIMAL (PLURAL)

- Hire a Sherpa _____ to guide you and your date on
  NOUN

  a climb of Mount _____.
  PLURAL NOUN

- Pick up your date in a chauffeured stretch _____
  NOUN

  and drive around looking at the lights of (the) _____.
  A PLACE

- Send a flying _____ up, up, and away into the wild blue
  NOUN

  _____ to skywrite: _____, *will you* _____
  NOUN   PERSON IN ROOM   VERB

  with me on a second date?

- Charter a/an _____ yacht for a swim at a private beach
  ADJECTIVE

  with the clearest, bluest _____ you've ever seen (clothing
  TYPE OF LIQUID

  and _____ are optional).
  PLURAL NOUN

MAD LIBS® is fun to play with friends, but you can also play it by yourself! To begin with, DO NOT look at the story on the page below. Fill in the blanks on this page with the words called for. Then, using the words you have selected, fill in the blank spaces in the story. Now you've created your own hilarious MAD LIBS® game!

PLURAL NOUN _____

ADJECTIVE _____

PERSON IN ROOM _____

SAME PERSON IN ROOM _____

PLURAL NOUN _____

ADVERB _____

PERSON IN ROOM _____

ADJECTIVE _____

NOUN _____

CELEBRITY _____

NOUN _____

ADJECTIVE _____

NOUN _____

PART OF THE BODY _____

NOUN _____

ADJECTIVE _____

NOUN _____

PART OF THE BODY (PLURAL) _____

VERB _____

ADJECTIVE _____

PART OF THE BODY _____

Adult MAD LIBS®
ROMANTIC FIRST-DATE MOVIES

The world's greatest *dating* game

Grab a tub of hot buttered _____ and treat your crush to
$\qquad$ PLURAL NOUN

the only things you *really* need for a great first date—you and one of

these _____ romantic comedy classics:
$\qquad$ ADJECTIVE

- *When Harry Met* _____: Harry and _____
  $\qquad$ PERSON IN ROOM $\qquad$ SAME PERSON IN ROOM

  have been best _____ for years before they realize they are
  $\qquad$ PLURAL NOUN

  totally and _____ in love!
  $\qquad$ ADVERB

- _____ *Maguire:* A/An _____ sports agent
  $\qquad$ PERSON IN ROOM $\qquad$ ADJECTIVE

  shows he has a conscience and gets fired. A lovely accountant

  and a/an _____-ball player named _____ who runs
  $\qquad$ NOUN $\qquad$ CELEBRITY

  around yelling "Show me the _____!" help him find his way.
  $\qquad$ NOUN

- _____ *Woman:* A billionaire _____ hires a hooker
  $\qquad$ ADJECTIVE $\qquad$ NOUN

  with a/an _____ of gold to keep him "company."
  $\qquad$ PART OF THE BODY

- *How to Lose a/an* _____ *in Ten Days:* A/An _____
  $\qquad$ NOUN $\qquad$ ADJECTIVE

  girl and a cute _____ do everything they can to get on
  $\qquad$ NOUN

  each other's last _____ as part of a bet.
  $\qquad$ PART OF THE BODY (PLURAL)

- _____ *Anything:* Five _____ words—boom box
  $\qquad$ VERB $\qquad$ ADJECTIVE

  over the _____. Enough said!
  $\qquad$ PART OF THE BODY

Adult MAD LIBS®

The world's greatest ___*sex*___ game

Kama Sutra Mad Libs

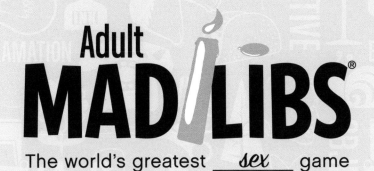

by Laura Marchesani

Mad Libs
An Imprint of Penguin Random House

MAD LIBS® is fun to play with friends, but you can also play it by yourself! To begin with, DO NOT look at the story on the page below. Fill in the blanks on this page with the words called for. Then, using the words you have selected, fill in the blank spaces in the story. Now you've created your own hilarious MAD LIBS® game!

ADJECTIVE _____

ADJECTIVE _____

NOUN _____

ADJECTIVE _____

PLURAL NOUN _____

NOUN _____

NUMBER _____

EXCLAMATION _____

PLURAL NOUN _____

VERB _____

ADJECTIVE _____

VERB _____

PART OF THE BODY (PLURAL) _____

ADJECTIVE _____

SILLY WORD _____

ADJECTIVE _____

ADJECTIVE _____

NOUN _____

The Kama Sutra is a/an _____ Indian Hindu text all about

ADJECTIVE

_____ intercourse! Despite what you may think, the Kama

ADJECTIVE

Sutra isn't just a/an _____ manual (though it can be used for

NOUN

that, too!). It's also a guide to how to live a/an _____ life.

ADJECTIVE

Many _____ believe that the _____ Sutra was written

PLURAL NOUN ⁣ NOUN

between 400 BCE and _____ CE. _____! Who knew

NUMBER ⁣ EXCLAMATION

our great-great-grand- _____ could _____ so well?

PLURAL NOUN ⁣ VERB

Some chapters in the Kama Sutra describe _____ lessons, like

ADJECTIVE

how to acquire and _____ a wife; how to caress, kiss, and bite

VERB

with your _____; and how to become friends with your

PART OF THE BODY (PLURAL)

exes (DON'T!). The Kama Sutra also covers the four _____

ADJECTIVE

goals of life: Dharma, Artha, Kama, and _____. Even if you're

SILLY WORD

reading it just for the _____ pictures, the Kama Sutra can also

ADJECTIVE

help you to become a more _____ person—in and out of the

ADJECTIVE

_____-room!

NOUN

Adult
MAD LIBS®
WATER SPORTS

The world's greatest _sex_ game

MAD LIBS® is fun to play with friends, but you can also play it by yourself! To begin with, DO NOT look at the story on the page below. Fill in the blanks on this page with the words called for. Then, using the words you have selected, fill in the blank spaces in the story. Now you've created your own hilarious MAD LIBS® game!

ADJECTIVE _____

NOUN _____

VERB ENDING IN "ING" _____

A PLACE _____

NOUN _____

ADJECTIVE _____

ADJECTIVE _____

PLURAL NOUN _____

NOUN _____

NOUN _____

PART OF THE BODY (PLURAL) _____

PART OF THE BODY (PLURAL) _____

NOUN _____

PART OF THE BODY (PLURAL) _____

VERB _____

Adult MAD LIBS®   WATER SPORTS

The world's greatest _sex_ game

If you want to keep things _____ with your longtime
                            ADJECTIVE

_____, you have to shake it up! Try moving your love-
      NOUN

_____ sessions outside of (the) _____ and into a
VERB ENDING IN "ING"   A PLACE

more aquatic _____: the bath! The phrase "_____
              NOUN   ADJECTIVE

when wet" has never sounded so _____! Here's a list of
                                ADJECTIVE

_____ to try:
PLURAL NOUN

Sea Horse: A lot like the reverse _____-girl, but
                                      NOUN

underwater. Giddyap!

Niagara Falls: Ask your _____ to massage your
                            NOUN

_____ from behind with soapy _____.
PART OF THE BODY (PLURAL)   PART OF THE BODY (PLURAL)

Hot-Tub Hug: Crouch on top of your _____ and use your
                                       NOUN

fingers to massage his _____ as you _____ up
                       PART OF THE BODY (PLURAL)   VERB

and down.

Adult MAD LIBS®

The world's greatest _sex_ game

THE RIGHT AND WRONG PLACES TO READ THE KAMA SUTRA

MAD LIBS® is fun to play with friends, but you can also play it by yourself! To begin with, DO NOT look at the story on the page below. Fill in the blanks on this page with the words called for. Then, using the words you have selected, fill in the blank spaces in the story. Now you've created your own hilarious MAD LIBS® game!

NOUN _____

ADJECTIVE _____

NOUN _____

NOUN _____

ADJECTIVE _____

ADJECTIVE _____

NOUN _____

NUMBER _____

NOUN _____

ADJECTIVE _____

NOUN _____

PLURAL NOUN _____

ADJECTIVE _____

NOUN _____

NOUN _____

ADJECTIVE _____

Adult MAD LIBS®

The world's greatest ___sex___ game

THE RIGHT AND WRONG PLACES TO READ THE KAMA SUTRA

Right: In your _____-room with your _____ partner
   NOUN   ADJECTIVE

Wrong: In your _____-room with someone who is not your
   NOUN

_____!
   NOUN

Right: Hidden inside a copy of *A/An* _____ *History of Time*
                                      ADJECTIVE

while riding _____ transportation
   ADJECTIVE

Wrong: While waiting to be called for _____ duty
   NOUN

Right: With _____ of your friends during a/an
   NUMBER

_____'s night in
   NOUN

Wrong: On the couch next to your boyfriend and his _____
   ADJECTIVE

friend while they play _____ *of Duty*
   NOUN

Right: In your _____'(s) basement after they go to sleep
   PLURAL NOUN

Wrong: While babysitting your _____ sister
   ADJECTIVE

Right: As _____-room reading material while you're sitting
   NOUN

on the _____
   NOUN

Wrong: In the _____ restroom at work!
   ADJECTIVE

Adult

The world's greatest __*sex*__ game

MAD LIBS® is fun to play with friends, but you can also play it by yourself! To begin with, DO NOT look at the story on the page below. Fill in the blanks on this page with the words called for. Then, using the words you have selected, fill in the blank spaces in the story. Now you've created your own hilarious MAD LIBS® game!

NUMBER _____

VERB _____

ADJECTIVE _____

PLURAL NOUN _____

ADJECTIVE _____

PART OF THE BODY_____

ADJECTIVE _____

VERB ENDING IN "ING"_____

PLURAL NOUN _____

ANIMAL _____

NOUN _____

ANIMAL _____

PART OF THE BODY (PLURAL) _____

ADJECTIVE _____

Adult MAD LIBS®

The world's greatest __sex__ game

WHAT'S YOUR POSITION? PART ONE

The Kama Sutra lists _____ different ways to _____.
<small>NUMBER</small>   <small>VERB</small>

Grab a/an _____ partner and pick one of the following
<small>ADJECTIVE</small>

_____ for a/an _____ time!
<small>PLURAL NOUN</small>   <small>ADJECTIVE</small>

Fixing of a Nail: When a woman places one of her legs on a

man's _____ and stretches the other out. Practice makes
<small>PART OF THE BODY</small>

_____!
<small>ADJECTIVE</small>

United Congress: When a man enjoys _____ with two
<small>VERB ENDING IN "ING"</small>

_____ at the same time. Lucky _____!
<small>PLURAL NOUN</small>   <small>ANIMAL</small>

Congress of a Cow: When a woman gets on all fours and a/an

_____ mounts her like a/an _____.
<small>NOUN</small>   <small>ANIMAL</small>

Yawning Position: When a woman places both of her _____
<small>PART OF THE BODY (PLURAL)</small>

on a man's shoulders. It may be called "Yawning," but it's anything but

_____!
<small>ADJECTIVE</small>

Adult MAD LIBS®

THE ART OF KISSING

MAD LIBS® is fun to play with friends, but you can also play it by yourself! To begin with, DO NOT look at the story on the page below. Fill in the blanks on this page with the words called for. Then, using the words you have selected, fill in the blank spaces in the story. Now you've created your own hilarious MAD LIBS® game!

ADJECTIVE _____

NOUN _____

NUMBER _____

ADJECTIVE _____

PART OF THE BODY (PLURAL) _____

VERB ENDING IN "ING" _____

NUMBER _____

PART OF THE BODY (PLURAL) _____

NOUN _____

PART OF THE BODY _____

NOUN _____

ADJECTIVE _____

NOUN _____

NOUN _____

NOUN _____

ADJECTIVE _____

Adult MAD LIBS®

THE ART OF KISSING

The world's greatest __sex__ game

According to the Kama Sutra, one of the most _____

ADJECTIVE

aspects of _____-making is kissing. You may think that you

NOUN

outgrew kissing when you were _____ years old, but think

NUMBER

again. The secret to _____ sex is to understand that locking

ADJECTIVE

_____ is just as important as _____! There are

PART OF THE BODY (PLURAL)   _VERB ENDING IN "ING"_

_____ types of kissing described in the Kama Sutra. There's

NUMBER

the straight kiss, where two sets of _____ are brought

PART OF THE BODY (PLURAL)

into direct contact. Consider this your foundation! There's *the turned*

kiss, where one _____ holds the head and _____

NOUN   _PART OF THE BODY_

of the other _____ and turns them up for a/an _____

NOUN   _ADJECTIVE_

smooch. *The kiss that awakens* happens when a/an _____

NOUN

kisses a woman who is asleep—or pretending to be asleep—in her

_____. Just be careful of morning _____! Kissing:

NOUN   _NOUN_

easy to learn, _____ to master!

ADJECTIVE

MAD LIBS® is fun to play with friends, but you can also play it by yourself! To begin with, DO NOT look at the story on the page below. Fill in the blanks on this page with the words called for. Then, using the words you have selected, fill in the blank spaces in the story. Now you've created your own hilarious MAD LIBS® game!

ADJECTIVE _____

NOUN _____

ADJECTIVE _____

NOUN _____

ADJECTIVE _____

A PLACE _____

ADJECTIVE _____

PART OF THE BODY _____

ADJECTIVE _____

PLURAL NOUN _____

TYPE OF FOOD _____

VERB ENDING IN "ING" _____

PART OF THE BODY _____

ADJECTIVE _____

NOUN _____

ADJECTIVE _____

Adult MAD LIBS®

KAMA SUTRA SHOPPING LIST

The world's greatest __sex__ game

You've got a/an _____ date tonight with your _____
ADJECTIVE   _NOUN_

of the month and you're hoping to get _____. If you want
ADJECTIVE

to show your _____ a great time, you'd better make sure
NOUN

to pick up these _____ items on your next trip to (the)
ADJECTIVE

_____:
A PLACE

- Massage candle: Adds a/an _____ glow to the bedroom . . .
  ADJECTIVE

  and gives you an excuse to touch your date's _____.
  PART OF THE BODY

- Arousal gel: Makes a woman so _____, she can't control
  ADJECTIVE

  her _____!
  PLURAL NOUN

- _____-flavored condom: Gives new meaning to the
  TYPE OF FOOD

  phrase "_____ out."
  VERB ENDING IN "ING"

- Vibrating _____ ring: Guarantees a/an _____
  PART OF THE BODY   _ADJECTIVE_

  finish for both man and _____.
  NOUN

- Scented bath gel: So you can both get clean after you've gotten all

  _____!
  ADJECTIVE

Adult
MAD LIBS®

REQUIRED READING

The world's greatest _sex_ game

MAD LIBS® is fun to play with friends, but you can also play it by yourself! To begin with, DO NOT look at the story on the page below. Fill in the blanks on this page with the words called for. Then, using the words you have selected, fill in the blank spaces in the story. Now you've created your own hilarious MAD LIBS® game!

NUMBER _____

COLOR _____

NOUN _____

ADJECTIVE _____

NOUN _____

NOUN _____

ADJECTIVE _____

ADJECTIVE _____

ADJECTIVE _____

NOUN _____

PERSON IN ROOM _____

ADJECTIVE _____

VERB _____

NUMBER _____

NOUN _____

LETTER OF THE ALPHABET _____

Adult MAD LIBS®
The world's greatest ___sex___ game

REQUIRED READING

So you've read _____ *Shades of* _____—all three
NUMBER   COLOR

books in the series, in fact! Think that makes you a/an _____
                                                        NOUN

expert? Think again! There are tons of _____ books about
                                        ADJECTIVE

mastering the horizontal _____.
                          NOUN

The Kama Sutra: The only bible you'll need on your bedside

_____
NOUN

My Secret Garden: The _____ sister to *Fifty Shades of Grey,*
                        ADJECTIVE

all about secret _____ fantasies
                  ADJECTIVE

Fear of Flying: _____ for coining the term "zipless
                  ADJECTIVE

_____"
NOUN

Lady _____*'s Lover:* A book so _____, it was banned
       PERSON IN ROOM   ADJECTIVE

Lolita: Or, How to _____ a Minor
                      VERB

The _____ *Love Languages:* Says you can have better sex
       NUMBER

with your _____ if you understand how they communicate.
           NOUN

Anything for a big _____!
                    LETTER OF THE ALPHABET

MAD LIBS® is fun to play with friends, but you can also play it by yourself! To begin with, DO NOT look at the story on the page below. Fill in the blanks on this page with the words called for. Then, using the words you have selected, fill in the blank spaces in the story. Now you've created your own hilarious MAD LIBS® game!

ADJECTIVE _____

ARTICLE OF CLOTHING (PLURAL) _____

ANIMAL (PLURAL) _____

ADVERB _____

VERB _____

PART OF THE BODY _____

ADJECTIVE _____

VERB _____

NOUN _____

ADJECTIVE _____

ADJECTIVE _____

VERB _____

PART OF THE BODY _____

TYPE OF LIQUID _____

ADJECTIVE _____

TYPE OF FOOD _____

NOUN _____

Adult MAD LIBS® MOUTHING OFF

The world's greatest ___*sex*___ game

_____ sex is about so much more than taking off your
ADJECTIVE

_____ and screwing like _____! If you want to
ARTICLE OF CLOTHING (PLURAL)   ANIMAL (PLURAL)

_____ please your partner, learn how to make him or her
ADVERB

_____ using only your _____! Here are some tips
VERB   PART OF THE BODY

to make your trip down south much more _____:
                                              ADJECTIVE

1. _____ passionately. If you enjoy giving oral
   VERB

   _____ just as much as you enjoy receiving it, you'll never
   NOUN

   get _____!
        ADJECTIVE

2. Find out which areas are most _____ to your partner. If
                                      ADJECTIVE

   you don't know, ask! And don't be afraid to kiss and _____
                                                             VERB

   in unusual places, like his or her _____.
                                         PART OF THE BODY

3. Use lots of _____. If you're feeling _____, try
                 TYPE OF LIQUID   ADJECTIVE

   _____-flavored lube or whipped _____.
   TYPE OF FOOD   NOUN

Adult MAD LIBS®

WHAT'S YOUR POSITION?
PART TWO

The world's greatest __sex__ game

MAD LIBS® is fun to play with friends, but you can also play it by yourself! To begin with, DO NOT look at the story on the page below. Fill in the blanks on this page with the words called for. Then, using the words you have selected, fill in the blank spaces in the story. Now you've created your own hilarious MAD LIBS® game!

NOUN _____

ADJECTIVE _____

PART OF THE BODY (PLURAL) _____

VERB _____

VERB ENDING IN "ING" _____

ADJECTIVE _____

NUMBER _____

PART OF THE BODY (PLURAL) _____

ADJECTIVE _____

PART OF THE BODY _____

NOUN _____

NOUN _____

PART OF THE BODY (PLURAL) _____

ADJECTIVE _____

ADVERB _____

ADJECTIVE _____

Adult MAD LIBS®

WHAT'S YOUR POSITION? PART TWO

The world's greatest __sex__ game

Here are more positions to drive you and your _____

NOUN

_____!

ADJECTIVE

The Lower Union: The woman bends her knees and places her

_____ on the man's chest. This one is guaranteed to make

PART OF THE BODY (PLURAL)

you _____!

VERB

The Rest of the Warrior: Perfect for long, slow _____ after

VERB ENDING IN "ING"

a round of wild and _____ lovemaking. The woman lies on

ADJECTIVE

her back at a/an _____-degree angle to the man, with her

NUMBER

_____ over his side. This puts him in a/an _____

PART OF THE BODY (PLURAL)   ADJECTIVE

position to use his hands to play with her _____!

PART OF THE BODY

The Morning Star: Pull up a/an _____ and take a seat! The

NOUN

man sits on a/an _____ with the woman on top, facing away.

NOUN

The Position of the Tongs: The woman lays on her back and places

her _____ around the man like tongs. Put a couple of

PART OF THE BODY (PLURAL)

_____ pillows under the woman to _____ enjoy this

ADJECTIVE   ADVERB

_____ position!

ADJECTIVE

Adult MAD LIBS®

BE KIND, PLEASE REWIND

The world's greatest _sex_ game

MAD LIBS® is fun to play with friends, but you can also play it by yourself! To begin with, DO NOT look at the story on the page below. Fill in the blanks on this page with the words called for. Then, using the words you have selected, fill in the blank spaces in the story. Now you've created your own hilarious MAD LIBS® game!

VERB _____

TYPE OF FOOD _____

PLURAL NOUN _____

ADJECTIVE _____

NOUN _____

PERSON IN ROOM _____

ADJECTIVE _____

NOUN _____

NOUN _____

ADJECTIVE _____

NOUN _____

PART OF THE BODY (PLURAL) _____

PERSON IN ROOM _____

PART OF THE BODY _____

VERB _____

CELEBRITY _____

PERSON IN ROOM _____

ADJECTIVE _____

Adult MAD LIBS®

The world's greatest __sex__ game

BE KIND, PLEASE REWIND

Are you getting tired of reading about sex and don't have anyone to

_____ the real thing with? Grab a bowl of _____
VERB   TYPE OF FOOD

and pop one of these _____ into your DVD player for a
PLURAL NOUN

guaranteed _____ time:
ADJECTIVE

Ghost: You'll never look at your clay _____ the
NOUN

same way again.

Secretary: _____ Gyllenhaal at her most _____.
PERSON IN ROOM   ADJECTIVE

You'll want to break out your heels and _____ skirt.
NOUN

The Dreamers: There's so much nudity in this French

_____, don't watch it with anyone you might feel
NOUN

_____ around. That means you, Mom and _____!
ADJECTIVE   NOUN

_____ *Wide Shut:* In case you were wondering,
PART OF THE BODY (PLURAL)

_____ Cruise is not a robot and does, in fact,
PERSON IN ROOM

have a/an _____.
PART OF THE BODY

Gia: Just in case you want to _____ off to _____ naked.
VERB   CELEBRITY

Showgirls: Who knew _____ Spano had such a/an
PERSON IN ROOM

_____ body?!
ADJECTIVE

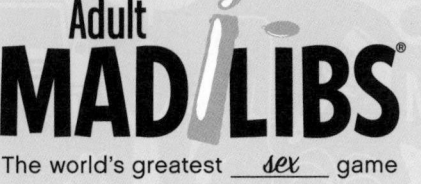

Adult MAD LIBS®

The world's greatest _sex_ game

BETTER THAN SEX?

MAD LIBS® is fun to play with friends, but you can also play it by yourself! To begin with, DO NOT look at the story on the page below. Fill in the blanks on this page with the words called for. Then, using the words you have selected, fill in the blank spaces in the story. Now you've created your own hilarious MAD LIBS® game!

SILLY WORD _____

ADJECTIVE _____

PLURAL NOUN _____

NOUN _____

PART OF THE BODY _____

ADJECTIVE _____

VERB ENDING IN "ING" _____

ADJECTIVE _____

ADJECTIVE _____

NOUN _____

VERB ENDING IN "ING" _____

ADJECTIVE _____

ADJECTIVE _____

ADJECTIVE _____

NOUN _____

ADJECTIVE _____

VERB ENDING IN "ING" _____

NUMBER _____

The Kama Sutra isn't just about sex, you _____! Sure,

<small>SILLY WORD</small>

learning all the positions is _____, but there are other

<small>ADJECTIVE</small>

important _____ to gain from reading the Kama Sutra.

<small>PLURAL NOUN</small>

So put away the _____-glide and tissues and give your

<small>NOUN</small>

_____ a workout for once! According to the Kama

<small>PART OF THE BODY</small>

Sutra, there are four _____ goals of life: Dharma, Artha,

<small>ADJECTIVE</small>

Kama, and Moksha. Dharma is _____ a virtuous life.

<small>VERB ENDING IN "ING"</small>

This is the most _____ goal of life—or at least it should

<small>ADJECTIVE</small>

be, you _____ _____-bag! The second goal of life

<small>ADJECTIVE</small>　　<small>NOUN</small>

is Artha, or _____ material possessions. Just don't be so

<small>VERB ENDING IN "ING"</small>

_____ that you sacrifice your Dharma! The third goal is

<small>ADJECTIVE</small>

Kama, or _____ erotic pleasure. Let's be _____—

<small>ADJECTIVE</small>　　　　　　<small>ADJECTIVE</small>

Kama is the reason why we picked up this _____ in the first

<small>NOUN</small>

place! Moksha is release from the _____ cycle of death and

<small>ADJECTIVE</small>

rebirth. There, now don't you feel smarter? You may now go back to

_____ off like a/an _____-year-old.

<small>VERB ENDING IN "ING"</small>　　　　　<small>NUMBER</small>

Adult MAD LIBS

OTHER USES FOR YOUR KAMA SUTRA

The world's greatest ___*sex*___ game

MAD LIBS® is fun to play with friends, but you can also play it by yourself! To begin with, DO NOT look at the story on the page below. Fill in the blanks on this page with the words called for. Then, using the words you have selected, fill in the blank spaces in the story. Now you've created your own hilarious MAD LIBS® game!

NOUN _____

ADJECTIVE _____

PLURAL NOUN _____

ADJECTIVE _____

ADJECTIVE _____

PLURAL NOUN _____

ADJECTIVE _____

ADJECTIVE _____

NOUN _____

NOUN _____

NOUN _____

ADJECTIVE _____

ADJECTIVE _____

PART OF THE BODY _____

ADJECTIVE _____

NOUN _____

ADJECTIVE _____

Adult MAD LIBS®

OTHER USES FOR YOUR KAMA SUTRA

The world's greatest __sex__ game

Have you read your _____ Sutra backward and forward,
NOUN

but can't seem to find a/an _____ partner to try out all
ADJECTIVE

the exciting _____ with? Even if you can't get laid, you
PLURAL NOUN

can still put your Kama Sutra to _____ use! The book is
ADJECTIVE

_____ and heavy, so use the pages to finally press those
ADJECTIVE

_____ from your _____ friend's wedding. Or use the
PLURAL NOUN   ADJECTIVE

book as storage for your _____ stamp collection or important
ADJECTIVE

documents, like your _____ certificate or Social Security
NOUN

_____. If you've got a/an _____ that just won't stay
NOUN   NOUN

open, the Kama Sutra makes a/an _____ doorstop. It's also
ADJECTIVE

a/an _____ weapon in case you have intruders—just hit
ADJECTIVE

them over the _____ with the book, and they'll be out
PART OF THE BODY

_____! Whatever you do, just don't throw the _____
ADJECTIVE   NOUN

away. You never know when you're going to get _____, and
ADJECTIVE

you might need a refresher!

From ADULT MAD LIBS®: Kama Sutra Mad Libs • Copyright © 2013 by Penguin Random House LLC.

Adult MAD LIBS®

The world's greatest _sex_ game

A TRIP TO THE ER

MAD LIBS® is fun to play with friends, but you can also play it by yourself! To begin with, DO NOT look at the story on the page below. Fill in the blanks on this page with the words called for. Then, using the words you have selected, fill in the blank spaces in the story. Now you've created your own hilarious MAD LIBS® game!

PLURAL NOUN _____

NOUN _____

ADJECTIVE _____

PART OF THE BODY _____

NOUN _____

NUMBER _____

NOUN _____

ADJECTIVE _____

NUMBER _____

PART OF THE BODY (PLURAL) _____

VERB _____

VERB _____

ADJECTIVE _____

VERB _____

Adult MAD LIBS®

The world's greatest __sex__ game

A TRIP TO THE ER

There are some _____ in the Kama Sutra that are guaranteed

PLURAL NOUN

to land you in the emergency _____. Unless you want to get

NOUN

_____ , be sure to avoid:

ADJECTIVE

The Suspended Congress: The man stands with his _____

PART OF THE BODY

against a wall and uses his hands to hold the woman up in a vertical

_____. Unless she weighs _____ pounds, it's not

NOUN — NUMBER

going to work!

The Yawning Position: This is the _____ that allows for

NOUN

the most _____ penetration. Problem is, the Kama Sutra

ADJECTIVE

was written _____ years ago, when men had much smaller

NUMBER

_____. Ladies, be warned—this one could _____!

PART OF THE BODY (PLURAL) — VERB

The Turning Position: A man and a woman _____ while

VERB

he turns her around in _____ circles. Try not to get dizzy

ADJECTIVE

and _____!

VERB

Adult
MAD LIBS®

The world's greatest ___*sex*___ game

LINGERIE FOR DUMMIES

MAD LIBS® is fun to play with friends, but you can also play it by yourself! To begin with, DO NOT look at the story on the page below. Fill in the blanks on this page with the words called for. Then, using the words you have selected, fill in the blank spaces in the story. Now you've created your own hilarious MAD LIBS® game!

ADVERB _____

ADJECTIVE _____

NOUN _____

ADJECTIVE _____

NOUN _____

PERSON IN ROOM _____

NOUN _____

ADJECTIVE _____

NOUN _____

PART OF THE BODY _____

ADJECTIVE _____

ADJECTIVE _____

VERB _____

VERB ENDING IN "ING" _____

ADJECTIVE _____

NOUN _____

ADJECTIVE _____

ADJECTIVE _____

Adult MAD LIBS® **LINGERIE FOR DUMMIES**

The world's greatest ___sex___ game

You've _____ memorized the Kama Sutra, and you're ready
            ADVERB

to get _____ and heavy with your _____-friend.
        ADJECTIVE   NOUN

There's only one thing missing—the perfect outfit for your night

of epic, _____ lovemaking. If you really want to get your
          ADJECTIVE

lover's _____ running, head to _____'s Secret
          NOUN   PERSON IN ROOM

and pick out the perfect _____ for the occasion. You can't
                          NOUN

lose with one of the following:

Babydoll: A short, _____ nightgown. Looks best when worn
                        ADJECTIVE

with a/an _____ or thong.
            NOUN

Corset: Suck in that _____! This _____ bodice
                          PART OF THE BODY   ADJECTIVE

gives you _____ curves—even if you can't _____
            ADJECTIVE   VERB

while wearing it.

French Maid: Not just for _____ up on Halloween! Just
                              VERB ENDING IN "ING"

don't be _____ when your lover asks you to clean the
          ADJECTIVE

_____ when you're done.
  NOUN

Garter Belt: Act out this _____ fantasy and dress up like
                              ADJECTIVE

a/an _____ secretary. Just add glasses to complete the look!
      ADJECTIVE

From ADULT MAD LIBS®: Kama Sutra Mad Libs • Copyright © 2013 by Penguin Random House LLC.

Adult MAD LIBS

KAMA SUTRA 2.0

The world's greatest __sex__ game

MAD LIBS® is fun to play with friends, but you can also play it by yourself! To begin with, DO NOT look at the story on the page below. Fill in the blanks on this page with the words called for. Then, using the words you have selected, fill in the blank spaces in the story. Now you've created your own hilarious MAD LIBS® game!

ADVERB _____

NUMBER _____

NOUN _____

ADVERB _____

ADJECTIVE _____

NUMBER _____

PLURAL NOUN _____

VERB (PAST TENSE) _____

VERB _____

ADJECTIVE _____

PLURAL NOUN _____

NOUN _____

PERSON IN ROOM _____

COLOR _____

NOUN _____

NOUN _____

Sex was _____ different when the Kama Sutra was written
ADVERB

_____ years ago. So what would the _____ Sutra be
NUMBER NOUN

like if it were written today? First of all, the writing is _____
ADVERB

confusing. You have to be a/an _____ genius to understand
ADJECTIVE

some of the concepts in the book! It would be much easier to

write the book as a series of tweets. Sex advice in _____
NUMBER

characters or less! Second of all, some of the _____ in the
PLURAL NOUN

book are totally outdated. Been there, _____ that! If you
VERB (PAST TENSE)

want to learn how to _____, you can just go online and
VERB

watch some _____ videos. To make an impact on today's
ADJECTIVE

_____, the Kama Sutra would have to feature _____
PLURAL NOUN NOUN

stars, like _____ Jameson and Sasha _____. Plus,
PERSON IN ROOM COLOR

the Kama Sutra really only covers sex between a man and a woman.

Today's Kama Sutra would totally include sex between a man and

a/an _____, a woman and a/an _____, and all of
NOUN NOUN

the above!

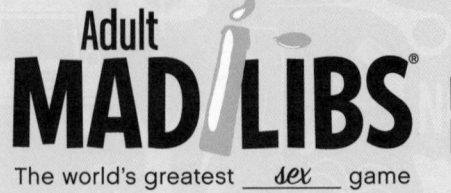

FOODS TO PUT YOU IN THE MOOD

The world's greatest _sex_ game

MAD LIBS® is fun to play with friends, but you can also play it by yourself! To begin with, DO NOT look at the story on the page below. Fill in the blanks on this page with the words called for. Then, using the words you have selected, fill in the blank spaces in the story. Now you've created your own hilarious MAD LIBS® game!

NOUN _____

ADJECTIVE _____

VERB _____

ADJECTIVE _____

PLURAL NOUN _____

ADJECTIVE _____

ADJECTIVE _____

NOUN _____

ADJECTIVE _____

NOUN _____

NOUN _____

ADJECTIVE _____

COLOR _____

ADJECTIVE _____

NOUN _____

Adult
MAD LIBS®

FOODS TO PUT YOU IN THE MOOD

The world's greatest ___sex___ game

You just finished reading the Kama Sutra and can't wait to invite

your _____ over for a/an _____ night in. Before you
     NOUN   ADJECTIVE

_____ into bed, serve a/an _____ meal that's sure to
  VERB   ADJECTIVE

get both of you in the mood for some _____!
                           PLURAL NOUN

Appetizer: Oysters on the _____ shell. This _____-
               ADJECTIVE   ADJECTIVE

known aphrodisiac contains zinc, which helps boost your _____.
                                         NOUN

Entrée: Seared _____ salmon. Oysters aren't the only
              ADJECTIVE

_____-food that will put you in the mood!
  NOUN

Dessert: _____-covered strawberries, preferably with
            NOUN

_____ stems to make it easier to feed each other.
 ADJECTIVE

Don't forget the _____ wine—the lower your inhibitions are,
                COLOR

the more _____ your _____-making will be!
        ADJECTIVE   NOUN

Adult
MAD LIBS®

The world's greatest _sex_ game

WHAT YOUR FAVORITE POSITION SAYS ABOUT YOU

MAD LIBS® is fun to play with friends, but you can also play it by yourself! To begin with, DO NOT look at the story on the page below. Fill in the blanks on this page with the words called for. Then, using the words you have selected, fill in the blank spaces in the story. Now you've created your own hilarious MAD LIBS® game!

NOUN _____

ADJECTIVE _____

NOUN _____

LETTER OF THE ALPHABET _____

ADJECTIVE _____

PART OF THE BODY _____

ANIMAL _____

VERB ENDING IN "ING" _____

ADJECTIVE _____

NOUN _____

VERB ENDING IN "ING" _____

ADVERB _____

VERB _____

NOUN _____

ADJECTIVE _____

ANIMAL _____

Adult
MAD LIBS®

The world's greatest ___sex___ game

WHAT YOUR FAVORITE POSITION SAYS ABOUT YOU

You've read the _____ Sutra backward and forward and have
NOUN

mastered all the _____ positions in the book. So what does
ADJECTIVE

your favorite _____ say about you?
NOUN

The Erotic _____: You enjoy _____ penetration—
LETTER OF THE ALPHABET   _ADJECTIVE_

and have incredible _____ strength!
PART OF THE BODY

The Rocking _____: You don't mind _____ up and
ANIMAL   _VERB ENDING IN "ING"_

down for long periods of time.

The Glowing Triangle: Triangles aren't just for _____ band
ADJECTIVE

geeks! But you may have played _____ in the high-school
NOUN

_____ band.
VERB ENDING IN "ING"

The Padlock: You love your partner so much, you _____
ADVERB

want to let them go!

The Slide: You own stock in Astro-_____ and petroleum
VERB

_____.
NOUN

The Ape: You're always up for a/an _____ challenge . . .
ADJECTIVE

especially when it comes to making love like a/an _____!
ANIMAL

Adult
MADLIBS®

The world's greatest ___sex___ game

GETTING IT ON IN THE GREAT OUTDOORS

MAD LIBS® is fun to play with friends, but you can also play it by yourself! To begin with, DO NOT look at the story on the page below. Fill in the blanks on this page with the words called for. Then, using the words you have selected, fill in the blank spaces in the story. Now you've created your own hilarious MAD LIBS® game!

ADJECTIVE _____

NOUN _____

NOUN _____

ADJECTIVE _____

VERB _____

NOUN _____

VERB ENDING IN "ING" _____

NOUN _____

ADJECTIVE _____

VERB _____

NOUN _____

PLURAL NOUN _____

ADJECTIVE _____

VERB ENDING IN "ING" _____

NOUN _____

PLURAL NOUN _____

ADJECTIVE _____

ADJECTIVE _____

Adult MAD LIBS®

GETTING IT ON IN THE GREAT OUTDOORS

The world's greatest __sex__ game

Is your relationship getting old and _____? Do you want
                                        ADJECTIVE

to turn up the _____ in your love life? Try taking your
                  NOUN

_____-making somewhere a little more public—the
    NOUN

_____ outdoors! Here's how to do it without getting caught:
  ADJECTIVE

1. You don't have to _____ far from home. Try pitching a/an
                          VERB

   _____ in your own backyard. This way, you have all the
      NOUN

   thrill of _____ outside, but no one can see you!
            VERB ENDING IN "ING"

2. Rent a/an _____ in a/an _____ hotel, ideally
                  NOUN   ADJECTIVE

   one on a high floor. _____ with your significant other up
                            VERB

   against the glass of the _____! Avoid this if you're afraid
                                NOUN

   of _____.
       PLURAL NOUN

3. If you're too _____ to actually rent a room, try
                      ADJECTIVE

   _____ in a single-stall restroom in the hotel's
      VERB ENDING IN "ING"

   _____.
       NOUN

4. Check out public places like _____ and beaches—just
                                    PLURAL NOUN

   wait until it's _____ at night and everyone is _____!
                    ADJECTIVE   ADJECTIVE

Adult
MAD LIBS®

The world's greatest ___*sex*___ game

GIRLS' NIGHT IN

MAD LIBS® is fun to play with friends, but you can also play it by yourself! To begin with, DO NOT look at the story on the page below. Fill in the blanks on this page with the words called for. Then, using the words you have selected, fill in the blank spaces in the story. Now you've created your own hilarious MAD LIBS® game!

NOUN _____

NOUN _____

NUMBER _____

ADJECTIVE _____

ADJECTIVE _____

ADJECTIVE _____

PLURAL NOUN _____

ADJECTIVE _____

PLURAL NOUN _____

NOUN _____

TYPE OF FOOD _____

NOUN _____

ADVERB _____

NOUN _____

ADJECTIVE _____

NOUN _____

NOUN _____

Adult MAD LIBS®
GIRLS' NIGHT IN

The world's greatest ___sex___ game

Everyone knows that the only _____ girls really talk about

NOUN

when they're together is sex! So grab your _____ Sutra and

NOUN

invite _____ of your most _____ girlfriends over

NUMBER · ADJECTIVE

for a/an _____ night in. To make it the most _____

ADJECTIVE · ADJECTIVE

night ever, you'll want to purchase everyone's favorite food and

_____. Try _____ finger foods, like veggies dipped in

PLURAL NOUN · ADJECTIVE

_____, and _____-friendly cocktails, like cosmos and

PLURAL NOUN · NOUN

_____-tinis. If you want to make it a/an _____

TYPE OF FOOD · NOUN

your friends will _____ forget, make it a/an _____ toy

ADVERB · NOUN

party! Talk about _____ vibrations! You'll have a ton of fun

ADJECTIVE

with your _____-friends and spice up your _____

NOUN · NOUN

life at the same time. No partner necessary!

Adult
MAD LIBS®

The world's greatest _sex_ game

HOW TO TELL IF YOUR PARTNER HAS READ THE KAMA SUTRA

MAD LIBS® is fun to play with friends, but you can also play it by yourself! To begin with, DO NOT look at the story on the page below. Fill in the blanks on this page with the words called for. Then, using the words you have selected, fill in the blank spaces in the story. Now you've created your own hilarious MAD LIBS® game!

ADJECTIVE _____

PLURAL NOUN _____

ADJECTIVE _____

NOUN _____

ADJECTIVE _____

ADJECTIVE _____

ADVERB _____

VERB ENDING IN "ING" _____

ADJECTIVE _____

PLURAL NOUN _____

VERB ENDING IN "ING" _____

NOUN _____

NOUN _____

ADJECTIVE _____

NOUN _____

VEHICLE _____

Adult
MAD LIBS®

The world's greatest _sex_ game

HOW TO TELL IF YOUR PARTNER HAS READ THE KAMA SUTRA

Sure, you may be _____ and proud about the fact that
ADJECTIVE

you've read the Kama Sutra and want to show it off to your potential

_____. But not everyone can be as _____ as you!
PLURAL NOUN _ADJECTIVE_

Here's how to tell if your _____ has read the Kama Sutra, too:
NOUN

- They try to impress you by telling you their Artha is _____.
ADJECTIVE

- They say their most _____ fantasy is _____
ADJECTIVE _ADVERB_

achieving the Suspended Congress.

- They ask you to pause in the middle of _____ so they can
VERB ENDING IN "ING"

reference something in their "_____ book."
ADJECTIVE

- They ask you to take yoga _____.
PLURAL NOUN

- They tell you their favorite part of last night was the _____
VERB ENDING IN "ING"

of the Bamboo.

- They try a different position every _____ and never do
NOUN

the same _____ twice.
NOUN

- They have a "Practice Makes _____" bumper _____
ADJECTIVE _NOUN_

on their _____.
VEHICLE

From ADULT MAD LIBS®: Kama Sutra Mad Libs • Copyright © 2013 by Penguin Random House LLC.

Adult
MAD LIBS® KARMA SUTRA

The world's greatest __sex__ game

MAD LIBS® is fun to play with friends, but you can also play it by yourself! To begin with, DO NOT look at the story on the page below. Fill in the blanks on this page with the words called for. Then, using the words you have selected, fill in the blank spaces in the story. Now you've created your own hilarious MAD LIBS® game!

ADVERB _____

NOUN _____

PLURAL NOUN _____

ADVERB _____

EXCLAMATION _____

VERB ENDING IN "ING" _____

NOUN _____

VERB _____

ADJECTIVE _____

NOUN _____

ADJECTIVE _____

PLURAL NOUN _____

PLURAL NOUN _____

VERB ENDING IN "ING" _____

ADJECTIVE _____

ADJECTIVE _____

ADJECTIVE _____

ADJECTIVE _____

Adult MAD LIBS® — KARMA SUTRA

The world's greatest ___*sex*___ game

By now you know _____ what the _____ Sutra is.
<small>ADVERB</small>   <small>NOUN</small>

But do you also know what *karma* sutra is? For one, it's a way to

describe the Hindu and Buddhist concept of karma, but in reference

to what happens to us between the _____. If you perform
<small>PLURAL NOUN</small>

_____ in bed, you can expect to have the same happen to
<small>ADVERB</small>

you in return. _____! Better start _____! This
<small>EXCLAMATION</small>   <small>VERB ENDING IN "ING"</small>

is especially true for oral _____. If you give it, expect to
<small>NOUN</small>

_____ it! Karma sutra also describes the _____
<small>VERB</small>   <small>ADJECTIVE</small>

repercussions that can sometimes come from being a hot and sexy

_____. If you rely on your _____ good looks your
<small>NOUN</small>   <small>ADJECTIVE</small>

whole life, there will come a time when _____ will no
<small>PLURAL NOUN</small>

longer care about you, because you've lost your _____! It's
<small>PLURAL NOUN</small>

karma sutra _____ up to you! Lesson is: Even if you're
<small>VERB ENDING IN "ING"</small>

_____, you still have to develop a/an _____
<small>ADJECTIVE</small>   <small>ADJECTIVE</small>

personality. Karma sutra may have a few _____ definitions,
<small>ADJECTIVE</small>

but don't be fooled: Some _____ idiots just don't know how
<small>ADJECTIVE</small>

to spell.

Download Mad Libs today!

Join the millions of Mad Libs fans
creating wacky and wonderful
stories on our apps!